JEAN and DINAH...

Who Have Been Locked Away In A World Famous Calypso Since 1956 Speak Their Minds Publicly

a LORDSTREET LiME

by TONY HALL

with Rhoma Spencer & Susan Sandiford
using the JOUVAY POPULAR THEATRE PROCESS.

Cover Design - Christopher Cozier
Dexter Lewis

Cover Photograph - Abigail Hadeed

ISBN: 0-7596-8796-X (e-book)
ISBN: 0-7596-8797-8 (Paperback)

This book is printed on acid free paper.

1stBooks - rev. 09/13/02

For JEAN, DINAH, ROSITA, CLEMENTINA, DOROTHY, BUBALUPS, STALLION, MARABUNTA, BLAKIE, ZANDOLIE, THE GLAMOUR BOYS. Especially THE MIGHTY SPARROW AND ALL THE OTHERS WITHOUT WHOM THIS WORK COULD NOT HAVE BEEN CREATED.

…to endure well
grief and mis-fortune and injustice
and then endure again…
- William Faulkner

jouvay - a community awakening.

DEDICATED TO THE MEMORY OF JEAN CLARKE

Praise for *Jean and Dinah*...

"Tony Hall's play *Jean and Dinah* . . . is one of the finest pieces of West Indian theatre I have seen in years-- it-- never surrenders its raw, poignant humour, its rhythm that mimics that of Carnival music, and when I saw it performed by two excellent actresses I felt continuous astonishment, delight and pride."

Derek Walcott, Nobel Laureate
Santa Cruz, March 8, 1997.

"It not only succeeds, it triumphs by committed, at times inspired acting and play and poise by Rhoma and Penelope Spencer."

Earl Lovelace, Novelist
Trinidad Sunday Express, December 11, 1994.

"Jean and Dinah is lively, amusing and often touching, with some powerful moments."

Judy Raymond, Journalist
Trinidad Express, December 7, 1994.

This script was developed with financial assistance from The Arts Support Alliance of Trinidad and Tobago (TASA).

The play was first performed on 29th November, 1994 at Planteurs Cocktail Lounge & Art Gallery, St. Vincent Street, Port of Spain Trinidad and Tobago,

with PENELOPE SPENCER as Jean
and RHOMA SPENCER as Dinah.

Research & Improvisation
- Rhoma Spencer and Susan Sandiford
Percussion - Tamba Gwindi
Set Design & Construction - Roger Hicks
Costume Design - Tessa Alexander
Stage Manager - Ken Joseph

Produced and directed by Tony Hall
for The Lordstreet Theatre Company
http://www.lordstreet.net
http://profiles.yahoo.com/lordstreet

The United States of America premiere was given on April 17, 1998 at the Goodwin Theatre, Austin Arts Center, Trinity College, Hartford, Connecticut.

Only the following was changed from the original Lordstreet Theatre production.

Set Design and Construction - Jeff Foye

Lighting Design - James Latzel

Produced by Jeffrey Walker - Austin Arts Center, Trinity College

Co-Sponsored by the Departments of Theatre & Dance and English, Trinity College and the Tourism and Industry Development Company of Trinidad & Tobago (TIDCO).

Special thanks to my wife Mary, my children Mauri and Lindsay, Lordstreet Projects Manager Naima Hay, Professor Milla Riggio and Dr. Arthur Feinsod.

CONTENTS

PROLOGUE The 1990's, Port of Spain, Trinidad.
A street.

ACT I The Preparation
Time: the 1990's.
Place: Dinah's apartment,
Port of Spain, Trinidad.

ACT II The Performance
Time: the 1950's
Place: a street and a hospital
in Port of Spain, Trinidad.

EPILOGUE The 1990's, Port of Spain, Trinidad.
Dinah's apartment.

"Jean and Dinah..."

Well, the girls in town feeling bad
No more Yankees in Trinidad
They going to close down the base for good
Them girls have to make out how they could
Well is now they park up in town
In for a penny, in for a pound
Yes it's competition for so
Trouble in town when the price drop low.

CHORUS
So when you bounce up Jean and Dinah
Rosita and Clementina
Round the corner posing
Bet your life is something they selling
And if you catch them broken
You can get it all for nothing
Don't make no row
The Yankees gone, Sparrow take over now.

Steelband Clash

Miss Mary

Drunk & Disorderly

INTRODUCTION
by Pat Ganase

Jean and Dinah,
Rosita and Clementina,
Round the corner posing,
Bet your life is something they selling…

The Mighty Sparrow sang this calypso in 1956 - the year of the ascension to government of the People's National Movement led by Eric Williams - and won the Calypso Crown. In so doing, he immortalised, freezing as unchangeably as if it had been done on film, these women of the streets.

No one knows about Dinah. She is dead, says Jean who is now 56, a plump aging crone, with a wizened right arm, the result of another legendary steelband clash. She looks older than her years. There are scars on her back. But her eyes are sharp steely points, though red-rimmed and sad. There's nothing happy about her until she starts to talk about her grand daughter, the child of her son who is in goal; serving time for holding up the neighbourhood drugstore, the same all-night operation that Jean depended on for milk or medication, bringing up her four children alone. "How he could do that?" she wonders angrily. "Imagine, rob a friend!" Everything she did, she did for her children she says. She had to get a confirmation dress for her daughter, she worked for it. And her story, harsh and unromantic, has formed the basis for the dramatic work by Tony Hall with research and improvisations by Rhoma Spencer and Susan Sandiford in their "Jean and Dinah speak their minds publicly…" Tony Hall says, "I never intended to be a playwright…but I slowly started to understand there was a special theatre to be crafted out of my Caribbean island experience, out of Trinidad and Tobago's history, out of the Caribbean people's cultural forms and expressions."

Growing up in San Fernando in the home of his schoolmaster father, Michael K. Hall, he learned life from the "people of the street", beggars, prostitutes and all. It was an education that was to inform his life choices: social action theatre, community television and The Jouvay Popular Theatre Process which he describes as an "awakening to the importance of our theatre of confrontation and participation".

The women, who created the roles of Jean and Dinah…who have been locked away in a world famous calypso, since 1956, speak their minds publicly, Rhoma Spencer and Susan Sandiford, brought their sensibilities as professional actresses and theatre students to the process. Both are "middle Trinidadian" women. Both work in the public service. They did the research, they found the old women, got into their lives. More than that, however, they brought their instincts and experiences as women, inheritors of the feminist legacy of the "jamette proud women driven by harsh economic and social conditions to be dancers and flagwomen, stickfighters. They would be the feminist spokeswomen of our time," according to Hall.

The play itself brings us up-to-date with the lives of Jean and Dinah. Dinah is old, ill, dying. It is Carnival Monday. Jean comes to rally her for one more j'ouvert (jouvay) morning jump up with the steelband, to play mas (masquerade) to play sailor. Dinah won't go. Jean won't leave her. Time reels back: they see themselves, their choices and encounters of the past 40 years. Dinah dies, but she and Jean know the truth about the incident that separated them.

January 1995

PROLOGUE

"To hell with the clock, I done hear the cock."
- Superblue

Throughout the prologue we hear a 'live' recording of The Mighty Sparrow singing the calypso "Jean and Dinah..." at the Dimanche Gras Show, Trinidad Carnival 1956.

Jean is 56 years old and looks in good health for her years.

She is downstage right, facing the audience (They become her mirror). She is putting on her makeup in an oval shaped mirror of light. She likes bright colours and likes to look bright and alive. We should get the feeling of someone creating a bright and alive mask. Her eyes, cheeks, lips, temples, eyelashes, eyebrows, hair and chin - using one hand she goes over all these parts very delicately. The other hand is crippled. She has a large travelling bag at her side. Once she is prepared she picks up the bag and walks very deliberately across the front of the stage towards stage left into subdued light. This should feel like a stylised jamette performance. It should have plenty of air to it - an inflated performance.

We hear a cock crowing. As the cock crows, Jean's mirror fades.

Dinah, who is upstage left of centre, gets up to sit on her bed (on a slightly raised platform). She lights a candle.

Jean stands in the semi-darkness downstage left and lights a cigarette. She draws on it and exhales. A smoke screen.

Dinah coughs a deep guttural cough that puts her candle light out.

Jean puts the cigarette out under her feet.

Dinah turns slowly, almost painfully and goes back to sleep on her bed.

Jean turns and walks upstage towards her.

FADE

ACT1

The Preparation

Darkness. There is a sound of steel. The sound comes from the rhythm section (the engine room) of the steelband. The sound is energetic, almost hysterical, as though something is about to happen. This is a sound that will occur throughout the play. The sound of clashing steel. Steel against steel. A cold hard sound and yet it is musical. It is syncopation.

We see a shaft of light as if through a door ajar. Daybreak. Inside is dark. Jean stands by the doorway. Dinah stirs. Dinah is 64 years old and not in good health. Her apartment is in total disarray, clothes everywhere, shoes, etc. Prominently displayed on her wall, there is an aging photograph of the late Honourable Dr. Eric Williams, the first Prime Minister of Trinidad and Tobago. There is a musty smell. The apartment has not been cleaned for some time. The sound of steel dies.

DINAH: Jean?

JEAN: You know what day it is! (*Pause.*)
And you ent wake up yet?

(*Jean starts to take things out of her bag. Pieces of costume, a bottle of rum etc... Dinah starts to cough.*)

JEAN: You know what day it is? Eh? Eh! (*Pause.*) You want some coffee?

(*Holding up the bottle, she goes off stage to make the coffee. Dinah coughs.*)

DINAH: What is the time?

JEAN (*off stage.*): Time to wake up, high time to get up off your black arse…

(*Jean returns and busies herself clearing up Dinah's room. She is laying out pieces of costume, getting ready to change into her own costume. There are many coloured pieces of cloth, etc. on the floor. She sets out a flag. Flag stick.*)

DINAH (*She sits up quietly.*): Jean you…

JEAN: Dinah, we late you know. (*Slight pause.*)

DINAH: Give me some coffee.

JEAN (*She steps over some things and goes off to get the coffee.*):

In the meantime get up and get yourself ready. I put out a few things already. We want to catch the bright noonday sun, remember?

DINAH: Jean, you remember the time when…

(*Jean appears with a cup of coffee and stands over Dinah.*)

JEAN: Dinah, we have no time for that now you know? (*She hands her the coffee.*) Okay? We done late already. It have all kinds of people on the road these days.

(*Jean starts to undress and then puts on her costume, her hands are in the air. Her face is covered by her bodice.*)

DINAH: Jean, remember the time you did come to me inside Lucky Jordan running…?

JEAN: Not now, oh God, not now, Dinah. You know what day it is?

(*She gets the bodice off. She is in a bra alone.*) Today is celebration day, Dinah. Celebration time, oh God!

DINAH: Is me, Jean. The man wanted to chop you. And is to me you did come looking to…

JEAN: What? That little poowatee man? He? The problem with he was he wanted a little screw and a little feel up balls for a little five cents.

DINAH: Jean.

JEAN: And, I wasn't paying he no mind, you understand…?

DINAH: Jean.

JEAN: Look at the class of woman I am. That is a little piss'n tail man. Eh? A little piss'n tail man. I didn't want to have nothing to do with he and every time he see me he want to insult me. When I see he, I used to spit on he…

DINAH: And why your hand so? Jean, why…?

JEAN: I use to haawk and sssspit on he.

DINAH: That is why he chop you. (*She turns and goes back to bed.*)

JEAN: And he do time, too. He do plenty time and he get chop back too. Look Dinah, why we talking this today, eh? Oh shit, man, get up nuh. And let us go down the road.

DINAH: And you do plenty time too.

JEAN: What you say? What is that you say? Look he get chop back, he get his arse chop back.

DINAH (*To herself.*): Wasn't you. Wasn't you.

JEAN: Eh? Was them boys and them in the band. I send them in he tail.

DINAH (*To herself.*): You too lie.

JEAN: He had to get it in he arse. Because, yes. I stand up just so and talking to them girls in the shop. Ma Popo was behind the counter. And I there talking good, good, good. Eh? And all I hear is, LOOK OUT!

DINAH: Oh God! (*She sits up.*) (*Pause.*)

JEAN: And as I do so. (*She screams.*)

DINAH: That was it.

JEAN: This is the hand, you know. This is the hand.

DINAH: So tell me something. *(She sips the coffee.)* What ever become of he now, girl?

JEAN: He arse dead, nah. Dead like a semp. (*Pause.*) Is six months I nearly dead in that blasted hospital, six months, six blasted months. (*Pause.*) Dinah, we ent have time for this now, you know. Look how you have me talking. Come, get up, and let us go, nah man. (*She busies herself with a piece of her sailor suit.*)

DINAH: Child, I lie down here thinking how such a big set of man just come to nothing. Ah hear he come out of jail and he was nothing.

JEAN: He must be nothing. He must be nothing. Is a woman energy he take, you know.

(*Dinah begins to cough. Jean has to help her to a sip of the coffee.*)

DINAH: No, bring water. Bring ice-cold water for me. (*Jean hurries out to get the water.*)

JEAN: What ice-cold water? You have fridge? You see what I mean. We could be down the road long time now. Enjoying we self. Enjoying we self. (*She returns with a glass of water and pacifies Dinah who by this time is almost out of breath.*) Okay, okay. Let us go now, okay? You taking tablets, right? (*Dinah shakes her head.*) Good. (*Pause.*)

DINAH: And he was a real good chantuelle, you hear, you talk about throat.

JEAN: Yes, man, when he hit you. (*She sings and gets more and more frenzied.*)

Out in the road
Come out in the road
Warrior

Remember that…

Out in the road
Come out in the road
Warrior

Ah seeing him and ah remembering the chop and he taking my energy.

Ah seeing him dancing and is like I can't dance. Dinah, Dinah, today is my day Dinah, he arse dead. Eh! Dinah, come Dinah.

Out in the road.

Come out in the road
Warrior
Come out in the road
Warrior
Come out in the road
Dinah
Come out in the road
Dinah

She sings this repeatedly. In the meantime it is as if the song was directed at Dinah. She has miraculously gotten out of bed and begins to dance with Jean who has taken up a stick and is charging around the room. It becomes energetic as Jean remembers the particular day and the particular man. Dinah has a stick in her hand and Jean sees her dancing. They are doing the Calinda dance. Jean stops. She relaxes.

JEAN: So you ready to go now. (*Pause.*) Come take a bath, you will feel better.

You want to take a bath? Eh? Come, let us go. (*Dinah goes towards the bed, she stumbles and falls on the bed. Jean hurries over to her.*) Let us go nah, Dinah. Let us go.

DINAH (*She organises herself on the bed in a half sitting position.*): They take all my energy, girl. They take a woman energy.

JEAN (*Sings quietly.*):

Joe Pringé, lend meh your bois to play
Joe Pringé, lend meh your bois, I say…

Joe Pringé…

DINAH: Jean.

JEAN (*Continues to sing. Dinah sings along with her.*):
Joe Pringé, lend meh your bois to play
Joe Pringé, lend meh your bois, I say…

DINAH: Ah could see my father in the ring now. He had a particular crouch as soon as they put a stick in his hand. And coulda move! Faster than lightening.

JEAN: Joe Pringé was your father?

DINAH: Shiffer.

JEAN: Who Shiffer, that?

DINAH: Shiffer Brathwaite, girl.

JEAN: Shiffer Brathwaite, boy.

DINAH: The man was tall and black. He use to look like he come straight from Africa just to fight stick. He was the champ in Freeport for years. They use to come from all over to Freeport to fight Shiffer. They coulda never touch him. He was too fast. You ever hear about the great Moscobee and Cutaway Rimbeau? Ah hear dem was men who coulda commit delicate surgery in the ring. Shiffer was in that class. (*Pause. She laughs.*)

JEAN: And is how you learn stick?

DINAH: My father use to say Man Man is a warrior who walk from Africa. He use to call himself Man Man. No slave ship for him, he walk for his own self, with his own two foot. And Ma would shout out from the yard, "What stupidness you telling the children? They will get licks in school for telling them stories". (*Pause.*)

(*Sings.*) Mooma, mooma,
Your son in the grave already
Your son in the grave already
Take a towel and band your belly. (*Repeat.*)

Ever since I was six, or seven, every time I hear the drums, something funny does run through my body. A shiver. A shiver. The first time he take me to the gayelle, well boy. It was like magic. I never see a place like that. It was the same street corner I did know, the same old junction in Freeport. But somehow with the men on the drums under flambeau light in one corner, the fighters with their head ties and stick blazing and chants chanting, I couldn't keep my head on straight.

And is like from that day to this… I don't know. I remember once in the darkness on the junction, just before he jump in the ring, my father turn to me and say, "But like you is a warrior too?" That day I feel a heat run through my body. (*Pause.*) From the time I was ten everybody know me dancing stick, sometimes with man, sometimes with woman. And my mother never say nothing, she always just watch me with them sad eyes. The same sad eyes she kept for Shiffer. She couldn't stop it. (*Pause.*)

JEAN (*Momentarily she is enthralled by the story, then she gets up.*):
Dinah, we done late already. (*Dinah sits staring.*)

DINAH: One day he was out in the bush.

JEAN (*Stops.*): Who?

DINAH: Sometimes he went out for days to hunt. That night when he come back he had a limp and only one dog. He looked green and he said a snake bite him. He suck out the poison and fall asleep in the grass. Ma start to say how she dream the night before. She see the sign, a white spider. In her dream she tried to kill it, stamping it with her foot tangled in the web. But it wouldn't die. It just looked at her and laughed with its pink gums and red beaming eyes. Ma, shut up! (*Pause.*)

Pa ent say nothing. He just went and took down his bois and limped out of the house, down the road. The dog running behind him. Ma stay quiet. I jumped up and shouted, No! No! My younger sisters watched and laughed and run out the back door. I was sixteen. I follow him. When I see him in the Rum Shop he was sitting on a stool with his head resting on the counter.

Ram behind the counter telling him if he sick he better go home, pushing another petit quart of rum and a clean glass in front of his face. (Pause.)

That night some young boy ride in the port and issue a challenge to all the old batoniers and them. Shiffer couldn't stop himself. He spring in the gayelle. The drummers crack keg, but Shiffer was carrying snake poison and he didn't see where that young bois come from. That was it. It lay him out flat, flat. The men lift him, they take him to the hole and he let out the blood. He never recover. He lie down home in the bed till he dead. We never know if it was from the snake bite or humiliation. He couldn't see the stick from the young boy. After that, things get hard. I had to help out. So I leave Arena, that is our part of Freeport, and come to town to look for work. All it had home was cane field and bush. (*Pause.*) And now look at me, I have no eyes.

JEAN: Dinah…(*Pause.*)

DINAH: They say it was Joe Pringé nephew. (*Pause.*)

(*Jean gets up and moves around the room organising Dinah's costume.*)

JEAN: Look, the sun hot…

DINAH: Oh God! (*Dinah turns and lies down in her bed.*)

JEAN (*She looks in disgust at Dinah.*): Cheups! (*She sucks her teeth.*)

DINAH (*Angrily.*): Let me tell you once and for all. You are a blasted jagabat and will be so all your life. I have my pride and I ent letting you drag my black, blind arse through the streets of Port-of Spain on this Carnival Monday for nobody, nobody, no focking body. You understand? I have my dignity.

JEAN: What is your problem? Dinah, what wrong? Today is our day.
If we don't play today, we might as well be dead.

DINAH: Listen to me. I played some of the best mas in this place. So you, nor nobody like you, can't tell me about mas. Mas is me and I is mas. And I am telling you that I am staying in my pissing bed, here today. (*She pulls herself under the covers.*)

JEAN: I don't know what wrong with you, nuh. You will let the whole day pass with this stupidness. I dunno…

DINAH (*Sitting up.*): Jean? Where you come from?

JEAN: How you mean, where I come from? Home.

DINAH (*From under the covers.*): You could go to fock back.

JEAN: Home? Where the fock is home? (*Pause.*) (*A caged bird.*) From the time I was ten, Uncle start to interfere with me. He come just so, early one Sunday morning when Aunty gone to church, and lie down on top of me on the bed. I jump up and push him off. I was always a fighter. My sister and them hear the commotion and they get up too. He say how he was looking for something he thought he leave in the room. Eh? (*Pause.*)

I used to have a wood dolly, make out of wood, hide up under my bed, since I was small. When I get bigger I didn't use to play with it no more. But it stay below the bed and I use to see it there all the time. All on a sudden, I miss my dolly. Two days later, I find the dolly by the latrine outside in the yard with the left hand break and the head rip off. When I look up so I see Uncle by the kitchen window watching me while he washing his mouth in the sink. I ent pay he no mind. That night he come back again. I tell him I go tell Aunty and he hold me tight, he cover my mouth, he was hurting me. He say if I tell Aunty he will kill me. He say I was a bad girl. I did hate he. I did real hate that man.

You know how much time I did feel to stab him, to poison his tea. (*Pause.*)

I didn't tell Aunty. When she came back from church? I didn't tell she nothing. This went on. 'Til one day, when I was thirteen or fourteen it hit me, this have to done. They had no money. (Pause.) I see my father once. They say he working on the American Base. I have to leave here. I have to leave this place and find him. And find my own way. My own money. These people can't help me. All they could do is fock me up.

Dinah, who has been under the covers for the whole story, uncovers herself and sits up. She starts to cough. Jean hands her the bottle of rum she brought with her. Dinah takes a swig and hands it back to Jean who takes a big swig herself.

A year after I leave there, I hear a truck knock him down off his bicycle and kill him. They say he was drunk. God don't sleep. (*She lights a cigarette.*) I use to lime with this dougla girl. Ahm…Elaine. She was from San Juan too. And she use to go to town regular. She was the one who invite me to come to the club in town, that first night, when I went. She was friends with everybody or, in fact, everybody was she friend. Anyway, we went by a table in the corner to have a drink. It was a kind of dark corner. (*Pause.*) And when she was drinking these two men came in the club. They wasn't

Yankee men or anything, they was local, jacket men. And them did know she, what she use to do. (*Pause.*) So, so they come by the table and we start to talk and thing. And what end up happening was that Elaine went with one of the men and I had it to go with the other of the men. And nobody never say nothing. That is how it start for me, and that is how I remember making my first set of money. Is a little while after I come to know you was in that club and had some weight with Popo and them.

DINAH: Yes.

JEAN (*She takes another swig from the bottle.*): That was the first money I ever make. I went and buy a yellow dress with the money, a pretty yellow dress, one with pleats. And I went to a dance. (*She gets up and starts to dance.*) All ah we meet by the abattoir and then we went up the road to the club. That was the first time I meet the Lord.

DINAH: What?

JEAN: Warlord, the calpysonian, nuh.

DINAH: That useless good for nothing. You know if you give them fellas a chance they will give you a bad name. They sing on you, just so. He and Little Sparrow. Next thing you know, people jumping to the tune of you on Carnival day.

JEAN: But you know in the early days he was good to me. As a little girl coming out I didn't know nothing. Is he who show me… but it was later when we was together he start to play the fool. He start to play up in his arse with that red woman. With she two long stringy foot.

DINAH: Is Warlord self who tell me is you.

JEAN: Warlord tell you what? Eh? What Warlord tell you? A day I pass by his house and when I pass by the house he wasn't expecting me. And ah see that bacra-Johnny gyal two red shoes on the step. (*Dinah starts to sing Blakie's "Steelband Clash".*) That bacra-Johnny gyal. Eh? He was lying down on the bed with, eh? With she two foot like two long string of bodi. Eh? Ah went in that house and ah pull out clothes, hear nah man, ah pull out clothes. And ah pull out clothes so and ah throw it in the yard. Eh? Want to play he leaving me for that half scorched, half scald, frigging magga head, red ooman, eh? Because she little redder than me. (*Dinah starts to laugh.*) What you laughing at?

DINAH: Red woman cursing red woman. They say she was Syrian.

JEAN: Syrian, my arse. Hear nah man. Ah take out he clothes. And ah throw he arse out in all he drawers. And then you know what ah do next? Eh? Ah take out my blue handle razor and ah stoop down and piss on it, on all he clothes. (*She uses the razor to prevent anybody from coming close to her to try to remove the clothes.*) You think he ever set eyes on a bacra-Johnny woman again? Eh? Not that calypsonian. (*Pause.*)

DINAH: You know when was the first time I hear about you?

JEAN: When was that?

DINAH: Them fellas, Lance and Leon and Janet gang come down in the club a night and say how police raid a fête up in San Juan. And how some young girl, who now come out, tell the police that she ent going down now, to check she next week. And she walk away like Brook Benton.

JEAN: You know, I don't know where I learn that from. Must be from Warlord and Marabunta and them. But I couldn't see myself in no Black Maria with my nice dress, what? And you know the rest of them just stand up there and watch me walk. (*Pause.*)

DINAH: They pick you up the next day, though.

JEAN: Yes. But I used to do them that well regular.

DINAH: Jean, why you didn't go back home when I talk to you, eh?

JEAN: Let us go into town nuh. You ent find we waste enough time with this nonsense.

DINAH: Yes, and look at us now. (*Pause.*) Why you come here? Why you don't go?

JEAN: You feel I can't go by myself? You feel I 'fraid? The road make to walk. I could fock well go and leave your arse right here to rot.

DINAH: Go home, Jean. Go home, it ent have nothing for you here. Go home.

(*Pause.*) And then you go and cut up Rosie. Lord.

JEAN: Dinah, why you bringing up all this today? Today of all days, Dinah?

Today is a day to forget. Today is a day when we could be anything we want to be. If we want to feel good Dinah, today we could feel good. Today we could forget and enjoy weself.

DINAH: I can't see my way to forget.

JEAN (*She takes another swig from the bottle which is near empty. She holds it up and looks at the low level.*): Shit!

(*She hands it to Dinah who smashes it out of her hand to the ground. The bottle breaks.*) What the fock you do that for? Eh? Why you do that? (*She goes for Dinah's throat to choke her. Dinah holds her off. Jean is on top of Dinah.*)

That was my last bottle, you focking old whore you.

DINAH (*Dinah gasps for breath.*): I never make a fares yet. You nastiness.

(*Jean is scared she may be killing Dinah and releases her.*)

JEAN: Oh, shit! Shit! Shit! Dinah you all right?

DINAH: How you mean if I alright? You was always a damn criminal.

I try my best with you all these years. Now you want to kill me.

JEAN: Dinah, Dinah, this is your fault. All now so we should be down the road playing we mas, happy, happy. Instead…

DINAH: You should be in jail. That is what. I should never let them let you out.

JEAN: It wasn't you. What you talking about? (*Pause.*) Eh? What you talking about?

(*Dinah turns to cover her head once again.*)

DINAH: For a pair of earrings, Jean?

JEAN: What causing this? What causing this?

DINAH: They never prove that Rosie take your earrings, you know.

JEAN: That was my gold earrings. Fourteen carat gold. They always want what I have.

Well, to arse with that. Everybody know that Rosie hand sticky. She always want to go with people man, take other people thing.

DINAH: So you cut her up. (*Dinah gets up*.)

She never recovered, Jean. She never recovered up to today.

JEAN: You don't take what is mines. I work hard for that. I have to look good.

DINAH: Rosita never look good again. And she use to look good…

JEAN: She was a old thief! (*She rushes to Dinah again*.)

DINAH: Wait! (*Dinah responds as if she can see. She is an old fighter. She gets up and throws Jean off her. Jean is thrown to the ground, skating across the room*.)

You see you! You is a jamette down to your focking heart. Ah not taking that, you know. Ah not taking that a-mother-cunt-all.

(*She pulls a white-handle razor from under her pillow*.)

I will slice your arse thin, thin, thin, right here and now. Make that the last time you jump me, you hear? (*Long pause*.)

You don't even know how you use to get out of jail. (*Pause*.)

You think is two hot water you put me in? Fock!

JEAN: Look Dinah, I…I… not taking no talk from nobody. You could say what you want.

People always jealous me, always. When you see I go into town and buy my nice shoe and my pretty cloth and come out, is so they does jealous me. And if I with a man, you can't be with the man. How you go be with the man? It must have fight. I go cut your arse, eh Dinah? I must cut your arse for that!

(*She lights a cigarette shakily after the encounter with Dinah. Dinah coughs uncontrollably, Jean tries to help with water, etc.*)

Let we go, nah girl. Your body not feeling for it? For the fête, girl. Let us go nah, Dinah.

DINAH (*Coughing some more.*): Too much smoke, girl. Is the smoke I can't take. (*More coughing.*)

Is the focking smoke I can't take.

JEAN (*Turning reluctantly, she takes a last puff of her cigarette and puts it out. She tries to busy herself with preparation of costumes.*):

I don't know why you getting on like this, nuh. You trying to spoil a good, good time yes. Look, Dinah, for the last time…

DINAH: Jean, remember when police use to raid the place. Popo use to get real vex.

Because he use to like to pretend that nothing going on in the place. But the first time police come. You remember how you come and hold on to me and you bawl down the place like twenty Tarzan.

JEAN: But I did know that you wouldn't let them carry me down so. So I did try a thing that first time. 'She is my mother and I am not in nothing. I just here'. And they did believe that before they get wind of me. And then finally they realise I was the little girl, the little red girl from San Juan. Yes, I not taking no talk from nobody, up to today.

DINAH: All you so use to give me real pressure, you hear. All the different girls. All you know the scene and, oh God! I used to want a little rest sometimes. But the police coming with some story. Bodi, that miserable, Syrian bitch, so she thin, so she full up with bacchanal and confusion. And "Bag of Iron", that ugly Bajan, only saying as a police he have he bounded duty. Always looking to lock up somebody. This time is only a little thing he wanted, yes. I remember a time he come up to me with his short pants and his two knock knee and say to me, "I want you to squeeze these".

JEAN (*In disbelief.*): Who is that "Bag a Lion"?

DINAH: Yes, "Bag of Iron" self! So I say, "You want me to squeeze these? You really want me to squeeze those? You better take out your balls and roll it…" He get vex and want to lock up the whole club. (*Laughter. Pause.*)

Jean? Jean? Why you choose here? Why you choose here? (*Pause.*)

JEAN: Dinah, look, ah fed up with you and this shit, you hear.

(*She busies herself as if she is about to leave. Dinah turns and goes under the covers again.*) You know I does vex for you. After all these years of making fares and…

DINAH: (*Jumping out from under the covers.*) Look, you don't wash your mouth on me.

You hear? You of all people. Not one of all you could point your hand in my face and say you see me making fares with any of the men inside here.

JEAN: Oh God, Dinah! Why you so hypocrite? You was to encourage…

DINAH: Me? You was to see me encourage? You make children but you don't make their mind. I was a waitress by trade and inclination. Popo and them entrust me into virtually running the place. Now the men and them has been very kind to me. (*Jean laughs out loudly, mocking her.*) And for your better information, if you want to know, is only the little striptease I uses to do in the clubs. In my heyday I did like my exotic dancing, a little limbo here, a little limbo there, fire-eating and so on. But you know, as I make child and thing I get this little belly so I done with that. (*Pause.*) So, if you know what good for you,

you better shut your damn blasted watery mouth. (*Jean stares at her.*) As there is a God above, (*Dinah makes the sign of the cross and kisses it.*) I never make a fares yet.

JEAN: Awright, awright, nuh. Why you always feel you better than people? What make you better than the rest of us? (*She blows smoke in Dinah's direction.*) You so full of focking shit. After all these years, insisting that you never make a fares yet. Everybody does laugh at you with that shit, Dinah. Everybody know is jackass talk, focking jackass talk. Everybody know that between you, "Winnie", "I Is A Whore Too", "Alice Sugar" and even "Big Six", all you probably make the most money out of all of us from the Yankees. Is true you must be give some money away, but all you lie down flat and make it. (*Laughs.*) Stand up too. I know that for sure.

DINAH: You know that for sure?

JEAN: Yes! For fock sure.

DINAH: Get to fock out. Leave my place now. Out! Out in the road!

JEAN (*Surprised.*): Awright, awright. You don't have to say it twice. I gone. Long time now I planning to leave you in this nasty hell-hole you living in. This nasty arse place here. When I gone, see who the arse will come and visit you in this rat hole.

DINAH: But Jean? Why you does come? Eh, tell me why? Why you come this time?

JEAN: To.........for we to play mas, you arse!

DINAH: Well, from now on stay to fock away.
I don't want to see you here again. You hear me?

JEAN: You ent have to say that twice you know, I gone.
(*She readies herself, packs things up quickly. With a cigarette in her mouth, she can only use one hand in her hurried action.*)

DINAH: Jean (*Pause.*) Why you pelt the bottle?

JEAN (*She stops at the door.*): Look, Dinah, let we go down the road and enjoy we self. You mean you go let Monday pass and we go still be here like two fools carrying on with this shit. (*Jean stands with the bundle in her hand not wanting to leave just so.*)

DINAH: Why you pelt the bottle, Jean?

JEAN: Dinah, me ent pelt no bottle, Dinah.

DINAH: We coming up Charlotte Street. As I say, Desperadoes coming up Charlotte Street, beating really sweet. San Juan All Stars coming down so, beating rather slow. Outside the Colonial Hospital, somebody say, "Look out!". Now, I didn't see who pelt the bottle eh, because they say, "Look out!". And you know what it is. When you hear "Look Out!", is to focking duck. Defend yourself.

JEAN: I ent pelt no bottle.

DINAH: Jean, Jean, everybody. Everybody saying is you. Ah don't know why after all these years that you wouldn't say that is you is the cause…

JEAN: Dinah, Dinah.

DINAH: …the cause why my eyesight…

JEAN: Dinah! Dinah!! I go watch you and pelt you and burst out your eye? Just so, Dinah?

DINAH: Jean, maybe you didn't mean to pelt focking me. But it hit focking me.

JEAN: Just so Dinah? Dinah, Dinah.

DINAH: Jean, everybody see you. Warlord.

JEAN: Dinah, fock Warlord. Dinah, Dinah. You not hearing me. Dinah, you are not hearing me. Dinah, I go watch you, you who I know so long….

DINAH: Awright, why you pelt? Everybody say…

JEAN: Who get house for you? Who get man for you? Who get work for you?

DINAH: Don't! You didn't get no man for me. I is a married ooman, you know. Don't bring me into your commess. I have five girl children in wedlock, in wed-lock.

JEAN: Oh God! You gone again. Where them, Dinah? Where the children? Why you so?

I go watch you just so you who I know so long and pelt you with a bottle and burst your eye, eh?

DINAH: Awright, Jean. You didn't pelt me with the bottle. You didn't pelt and burst my eye. But why you pelt the bottle, Jean? (Pause.) Jean, why you pelt the bottle? (*Pause.*) You can't answer me. You pelt a bottle, awright, it hit me…

JEAN: Dinah.

DINAH: You didn't mean to pelt a bottle to burst my eye. But you pelt a bottle. Why you pelt a bottle?

JEAN: I was holding on to my man in San Juan All Stars good, good. And you see me pelt bottle? What kind of bottle it was? Eh? Since you see so good, eh? What kind of focking bottle it was? Eh? Tell me that.

DINAH: A focking Eclipse bottle.

JEAN: I don't drink that, girl.

DINAH: And how you could be holding on to your man and waving flag?

You trying to mamaguy me or what?

JEAN: I never drink that, girl.

DINAH: Is the same man you did holding on to. Is the same man bottle you pelt. Is he bottle of rum.

JEAN: I don't drink Eclipse.

DINAH: I don't consult with what you was drinking. The man you was holding on to, he was drinking Mount Gay Eclipse. That is the rum everybody was drinking that time.

JEAN: So how I was waving the flag?

DINAH: Is you who tell me you was holding on to the man, you know, awright.

And if it is so, then is he bottle you had. Is he bottle you pelt.

And we didn't do all you nothing.

JEAN (*Pause.*): Dinah, all you was playing NOAH's ARK, right? And in the Ark had endless cutlash. What that was for, Dinah? Eh? To plant garden? Eh?

DINAH: You pelt a bottle and it hit my eye. (*Pause.*)
I spend my time in that hospital fighting to save my eye. You never come to visit me. Not once, Jean, not once. (*Pause.*)
Jean, why? Why Jean?

JEAN: Dinah, I didn't pelt no bottle, Dinah. Look at me in my eye, Dinah, I pelt any bottle?

DINAH: Jean, I can't see you. How I looking at you? How I going to see you?

JEAN: Look me in my eye and tell me I pelt a bottle. (*Pleading*)

DINAH (*Pause.*): Jean, what happen? You sorry, now. Eh? Jean, you is the reason and I don't know why after all these years you wouldn't own up. Jean, if you miss this one, that is it, you know. That is it.

JEAN: You know what day this is? What day it is?

DINAH: But let God be the judge.

JEAN: Dinah, you know what day it is?

DINAH: I don't want to know what day it is!

JEAN: You know what day it is?

DINAH: This day doesn't mean anything to me.

JEAN: You lie down there, Dinah.

DINAH: Jean look, I can't go on no more. My heart ain't good. Bubalups gone, I couldn't even go to the funeral. Ah hear nobody went. Now Mayfield up and gone. (*Pause.*) Where my five girls? Eh? Tell me this thing! (*Pause.*) If James was alive, God rest his soul. He was a good man. He had a good work. He worked in the Colonial Hospital and then when the People's National government come in, he had a party card and get a good work with Ministry of Works.

JEAN: Dinah, all you was always behind this politics thing. Where it get you?

This party thing and this Doctor Williams, eh?

DINAH: Don't talk thing you don't know about, child. When James hear it have meeting in the Square, he gone! He march in the rain when that same Doctor Eric Williams make the call to take back the Chaguaramas base from the Americans. Freedom for one and all! He even drag me and all along. They needed a flag woman. (*Pause.*) James was a good man.

JEAN: I did never like them People's Nationals peoples. They come up by me plenty times.

We went with them… by the bus load. The calypsonians sing. We get rum. I never trust them.

DINAH: I try my best with them children. I don't know what went wrong. Everybody always know what is your problem and could tell you about your problem. But I know I tried my best. It had one boy I adopt, that make it six children really. He working mechanic with Forde on the Eastern Main Road. But the girls and them, oh God! Jean you see them sometimes? Them children ent please my heart at all.

JEAN: I does see Katherine…

DINAH (*Jean lights a cigarette.*): I don't want to talk about it. I don't want to talk. (*Pause.*) (*Cough.*) And imagine we had a good, good house and that and all I lose… oh God…eh? (*Pause.*) (*Steel rhythm.*) What is that? You hearing something?

JEAN: No! What happening, Dinah?

DINAH: Like if ah hearing and seeing a steelband coming closer to me. It coming, Jean.

It coming straight for me. Jean, it bursting my head. Jean do something. Do something. Jean, Jean…

JEAN: Dinah, Dinah. (*Rhythm gets louder.*)

Dinah, I can't hear anything. Dinah, it is alright, is okay. Shit, Dinah, what happening? What happening?

(*Dinah covers her ears in the bed. Jean hugs her and tries to pacify her. The sound of pounding steel subsides. It cools down to a soothing rhythm before it dies completely.)* (*Long Pause.*)

Dinah, you awright? (*Pause.*)

(*Dinah sobs uncontrollably as Jean hugs her tightly.*) (*Long pause.*)

Dinah, what is…?

DINAH: Jean?

JEAN: Yes…

DINAH: What you was doing in San Juan All Stars? (*Jean moves away from Dinah.*)

You shoulda be with us, Marabuntas, Desperadoes. All the boys that we know on Duke Street by Lucky Jordan was in them band.

JEAN: Dinah, why you…?

DINAH: Jean, is that what cause the fight you know. (*Pause.*)

JEAN: Dinah, that is my business. My… (*Pause.*) …. focking business.

DINAH: You will never see. (*She turns and goes under the covers.*)

JEAN (*She continues to pack her things and goes towards to door.*):

You don't know how Harry use to beat me. And tell me all kinda things. He use to beat me bad, bad, bad. And he was with Elaine when he was with me. When the big girl died, he come around. I don't know for what. All these marks you see on my skin here, he is responsible. But I did real like the man. I did real like that man. (*Pause.*) When he drink he rum he use to tell me all kinda things, about how I having this man and that man. (*Pause.*) I couldn't complain to nobody, I didn't have nobody to complain to…..

DINAH: Jean

JEAN: Look, the Yankee I was to marry, Leroy father, did give me a slave band - gold, expensive. He always used to bring expensive thing every time he come. Harry take the thing and gone. You know I never get back that slave band my Yankee man give me. I never get back that slave band. I tell him keep it. It just right for him. It go blight he. One day he even plan-arse me. He beat me up with a three canal cutlash and tell me if I would only shut my cunt we would be better off. (*Pause.*)

He use to feel I was his property. But I was to get my freedom somehow and Carnival time was a time when I use to go on my own. Nobody could own me. Nobody could tie my foot that time.

DINAH: And that is when you went looking for Ramon.

That slippery Bound Coolie, his hair dripping with tallow grease.

JEAN: Ramon? Ramon wasn't no Indian. He was a Creole.

He use to like to slick his hair like the Warlord.

DINAH: Ramon wasn't an Indian?

JEAN: He had you fooled too. (*Pause.*) People use to take he for Indian or Spanish.

He was a good, good, man, you hear.

DINAH: They say he had a stick like Mastifé.

JEAN: Hush, nuh. With him I use to feel I could do anything, anything, anything.

Me and that man struggle together. I do work till I get the house down south. (*Pause.*) But the children was nothing like Ramon. The big girl, Dolores…

DINAH (*From under the covers.*):

But she wasn't Ramon child.

JEAN: No, that was Harry own. Worthless, just like he. She eventually went to the States and become a nurse. All my money. She was up there in New York nursing. She never send for me. And then she come and dead just so in a motor car accident up there. The car didn't see the lights. Same time Harry turn up by me asking if she ent leave nothing for he. Ah say: "Like what?". He say: "Well, you never know." Ah say: "Damn right, you never know." He did never know nothing. I use to hate to hear him say that. He use to say it all the time: "You never know". Ah feel he thought that was a joke. "You never know." And then he open his mouth wide, wide and laugh, a kinda horse laugh, *(Slight pause.)* arse hole, jackass. (*She starts to throw her clothes around the room.*)

DINAH: Jean.

JEAN: Arse holes. (*She starts to weep, pause.*) They let my baby bleed to death.

(*She slips to the floor in a sitting position and clutches herself tightly. She starts to rock.*) She didn't have to die. (*Pause.*) She was the first child with Ramon, a sweet angel. He did real like she. She was always quiet. Nice, nice child. Growing up good, good. She was only nineteen. Still young. She gone and pick up with these faith healers. Me ent know what it was. Some people say it was Witness. But if it was Witness, I woulda know it was Witness. I know a Witness when I see a Witness. (*Pause.*) Why she didn't go and have the operation? Ramon did know a good doctor fella in Brighton, who was willing to help out. Oh God! Oh God! Oh God! My baby bleed to death. She bleed to death, Dinah. Dinah, all I see is red. Red. Red! Dinah is that what kill Ramon, you know. He couldn't take it, Dinah. I had to be strong. I had to hold on for both of them. I had to hold on. (*Pause.*) After that, Ramon get small. All the energy went out of him. The spirit get weak. He take to going for long walks by himself. Then one day he disappear.

DINAH: And that was it.

JEAN: That was it. (*Pause.*) Then it was just me and small boy Toto alone, left in the house.

And you know Toto does look just like Ramon. Ramon in print. So Toto get everything. They say I spoil the child. But Dinah, he was all I had. With Ramon gone what ah go do? Eh? Tell meh nah, eh? (*Pause.*) All of a sudden, he start calling me jamette to my face. He and he little Junior Secondary hangman friends. I try with him and give him everything. By that time ah had was to go back to work. Next thing I know, I see he pick up with some white men, strange looking white people. They always just passing through.

DINAH (*She sits up in disbelief.*): Toto is a macomé man? (*Pause.*) I never realise…

JEAN: Well, me and he use to get away bad, bad… ah mean in we heyday we use to do we thing.

DINAH: We?

JEAN: But not like this. Oh God. No, not like this. (*Pause.*) We use to have some serious fight and on this day in particular he get vex…he went and get a big can of pitch oil…(*Pause.*) and burn down my house… I lose meh house…

(*Pause.*) I had no where to rest meh head...no where to rest meh head because of Toto. After all them years, Dinah, I had nobody...(*Pause.*) I never feel like if I ever love anybody.

DINAH: Eh, heh? (*Pause.*)

JEAN: Dis town have no love in it. Dis town never know what love is. And if Jean "In Town" say so, is so. Nobody know like I know. I did always want what I want. (*Pause.*) And look at me now, I old. I can't fix my teeth, the arthritis. And Cyril home there, he real miserable too, you know. He does help out, but he old in he arse...(*Pause.*) Dinah this is shit, man. I never carry on like this. This is real shit that going on here today. Dinah, like you put a spell on me or what? (*Jean jumps to her feet, energised.*) Dinah, you know what day it is, eh? Dinah, look I bring a sailor suit. You could play fancy sailor.

DINAH: Jean... let me.

JEAN: It have two piece of thing in the bag here. It have some sequins. It have some nice feathers. We could put it on it. And ah bring a socks. If you see socks, girl. Spit bring it from New York, is a New York socks. We go put it on. And you know what too, we go hold your cane. You see that cane you have there? Oh God! We go pretty that up. And ah have some spray paint. We go put pink and yellow and blue and it go look like a rainbow. Oh God, Dinah!

DINAH: Ah hearing it.

JEAN: Dinah, this year we go play a mas. We coming out with real fire. And when you hear you put that stick and you putting that thing on your head.

DINAH: Jean.

JEAN: Eh, Dinah?

DINAH: Jean, ah hearing, ah hearing…it….

JEAN: A teka, teka, teka, teka, teka, teka……

DINAH: Ah seeing them coming down the road…

JEAN: A teka, teka, teka, teka.

DINAH: Ah hearing the music…yes

JEAN: A teka, teka, teka, teka.

DINAH: What was the music? The road march? What was it? Ah hearing it.

JEAN (*Dancing and singing.*):
Drunk and Disorderly, meh friends and meh family…

DINAH: It wasn't that nah, nah.

JEAN: What it was? What it was?

DINAH: You know what it was, Jean! (*Pause.*)

JEAN: Dinah?

DINAH: Jean!

JEAN: You know what day it is? You know what day this is?

DINAH: Ah not hearing this day. Ah not hearing the day… that bitch, is he that tell me is you.

JEAN: The Warlord, nuh? Ever since the time with Bodi. And he did never like Ramon.

DINAH (*Starts to sing Blakie's "Steelband Clash".*):
Is a bacchanal, fifties' carnival, fête for so…

JEAN: You ent know what today is?

DINAH: Hush, husshhh (*Continues "Steelband Clash."*)

JEAN: Today is mas day. Come, come, let we try it on nuh, right?

(*Dinah sits up. She is spaced out.*) You hearing the music? Dinah, oui, Dinah… (*She starts to dance and sing "Drunk and Disorderly". She drowns out Dinah's "Steelband Clash".*)

DINAH: Oh God, Jean, that smoke, that smoke. (*She starts to cough.*)

JEAN: What you talking about? Dinah, come on!

DINAH: Eh? (*As if far away.*)

JEAN: What happen you can't hear or what? Dinah! You deaf now?

DINAH: Eh, heh.

JEAN: Dinah.

DINAH: What we playing? (*As if in a trance.*)

JEAN: We playing sailor. Ah tell you sailor already. And we go have a pretty kinda rainbow stick. Where your stick?

DINAH: What kinda sailor? Fancy Sailor?

JEAN: Rainbow sailor. (*Dinah gets up out of the bed.*) And we go drop so and drop so and drop so. Where yuh stick? We go seek revenge on dem glamour boys again. (*Dinah is up starting to dance by this time. Jean is in full flight.*) All Hands on Deck! Remember that band, Dinah? Where your stick? Bring your stick. Bring your stick, girl. (*Jean puts a stick into Dinah's hand.*) Get a stick. Get a flag. Get a man. Eh? A stick… (*They are both dancing and laughing and having a good time.*) And we gone. Look at we… heh, heh, heh, heh, heh. (*A delicate, energetic sailor heel-and toe- dance ensues.*) Remember when we use to move with Marabuntas, eh? With Desperadoes, eh? (*Dinah laughs. She stops dancing.*) You get up? You get up then?

DINAH: Yes

JEAN: We going and play, right? Let me get the bag and thing. Come. (*Pause.*) You going and bathe first?

DINAH: Cheups. (*She sucks her teeth.*)

JEAN: You bathing first?

DINAH: Nah.

JEAN: Dinah? What happen now?
(*Childish, as if to her mother.*)
You don't want to play sailor or what?
(*Near to tears.*)

DINAH (*Stumbles back to bed.*): Them days done, girl.

JEAN: You want to play Princess Anne? What happen?

DINAH: Them days done! Done! (*Pause.*)

JEAN: How you mean them days done?

DINAH: Is only de Lima and de Verteuil and them who…

JEAN: But now we could play that. We could play them.

DINAH (*Confused.*): Why? How? How?

JEAN: How you mean how? We will play them!

DINAH: We go play Queen? (*Like a little child. Jean puts on a cape and a tiara on Dinah. She hands her the rainbow stick.*)

JEAN (*Continues like a child.*): Yes, and I have my tiara and all kind of Queen thing from when I use to be Queen. We could use that and we go make you look pretty, pretty, pretty.

DINAH: Oh God, Jean. (*Dinah becomes a queen.*)

JEAN (*She struts like a queen, trying to keep Dinah up.*): We could play Queen.

Hear it now. Presenting Queen Dinah… (*Laughter. Dinah gets into it.*) ….of Lucky Jordan.

DINAH: Them French Creoles ent want nothing with we.

JEAN (*High accent.*): Nothing. Most definitely. They do not want anything to do with us. Most definitely…And now, sponsored by Ma and Pa Popo. Presenting, Miss Dinah!!!!!!! (*Dinah stands and starts to move forward. She stumbles into a piece of furniture and is guided by Jean. They both sing, "Valerie Valera".*) And there she goes, Ladies and Gentlemen. Doesn't she look splendid? A lusty round of applause for Princess Di…

DINAH (*She tries to speak properly.*): My name is Dinah Jordan Brathwaite, Braithwaithe, Jordon. (*Clears her throat.*) I am originally from Freeport. I am a Freeportian… ah… (*Laughter.*)

JEAN: Another lusty rounds of applause for this busty Freeport Queen.

(*Jean starts to sing the calypso, "Jean and Dinah".)*

DINAH (*Dancing forward, she sings.*): The Yankees gone and Dinah take over now…

JEAN: Come on…let's hear it for the Princess of Freeport… (*Applause.*)

FADE

END OF ACT I

ACT 2

The Performance

Bright sunshine. Jean and Dinah are thirty-five years younger, before Jean got her hand wound and Dinah lost her eye. They are dressed in white, worn sailor suits. The suits are not clean. They have been playing mas in them all day.

Most of Act II is played off-stage, close to the audience. It is performed as if on the street on Carnival day with an impromptu audience.

This opening sequence is a clown routine based on the movements and characteristics of the bad behaved sailor masquerade of the street. Jean holds a large shoebox in one hand and has a baby bottle, with rum and a nipple attached, hung around her neck. Dinah carries a stick (the rainbow stick prepared in Act 1) and a huge tin of talcum powder. She throws powder (as is the tradition) at the audience liberally from time to time to punctuate her speech. They have been drinking.

JEAN (*They enter singing.*): You see Miss Mary.

DINAH: One pound.

JEAN: She big and hairy.

DINAH: One pound.

JEAN: You see she mother.

DINAH: One pound.

JEAN: You see she father.

DINAH: One pound.

JEAN: For Carnival this year
I have Miss Mary here
Miss Mary weighing.

DINAH: One pound.

JEAN: So come and see she
(*Pointing to the shoebox, she gives a few audience members a peek in the box. In the box is the broken wooden dolly.*)

DINAH: One pound.
(*They end the song with a scandalous laugh.*)

JEAN: You ent see him? How he peeping?

DINAH: Yes. You ain't make out that…woman from…?

JEAN: Is she? That is the one who does be up by Lucky Jordan there? Is she? Is she? No.

DINAH: Heh? You know me? She look like she…
(*Jean & Dinah laugh with each other.*)

JEAN: It well look like she. Ah did burst she arse.

DINAH: Madam, sorry.

JEAN: Ah did burst she arse.

DINAH: I am very sorry.

JEAN: Is not she? The same woman arse who we burst.

DINAH: Oh gosh, hush, nah. (*Jean laughs.*) Good evening, (*to another member of the audience*) enjoying the show…? (*Pause.*)…Ah like your hair cut…You ever see a bald head with a part? (*Pause.*)…Check your bumsee. (*Laughter.*) You remember me?

JEAN: We play sailor. You can't remember?
You play sailor with Jean and Dinah…

DINAH: What you playing? He playing he can't remember we…

JEAN: Last year.

DINAH: You can't remember? A big old…

JEAN: Last year we play sailor, we playing sailor again this year. What happen, you don't want to play with we or what?

DINAH: Aye, aye, I will embarrass you here tonight. Don't play you don't know me, you know.

JEAN: You ent want to play sailor again?

DINAH: You accustom coming and make your fares on the Gaza Strip, you know… (*They laugh.*)

JEAN: Come, come, give we a little sailor, a little sailor thing. (*They dance some heel and toe and invite an audience member to dance with them. They encourage a white man to get up from the audience and dance with them.*) You know the thing. You know the thing. (*They dance for a while. Dinah throws powder on him. Laughter. He returns to his seat as they get the audience to give him a round of applause.*)

(*They sing*) You see Miss Mary.

DINAH: One pound. (*She uses her waist to good advantage.*)

JEAN: She fat and juicy. (*She gives an audience member a peek in the box.*)

DINAH: One pound.

JEAN: For Carnival this year, I have it right here.

JEAN & DINAH: Miss Mary weighing, one pound.

JEAN: So come and see she.

(*She gives another person a little peek. Laughter as they stop singing.*)

DINAH: But listen, I remember he you know.

JEAN: You remember he?

DINAH: Yeah.

JEAN: Which part? (*Laughter.*)

DINAH: It could be he. But it ent have to be he.

JEAN: Oh ho, Cyril.

DINAH: You resemble the man.

JEAN: Cyril who does come by me all the time. He look little bit like Cyril, you know.

DINAH: Your name is Cyril? You not Cyril? You is Cecil? (*Laughter.*)

JEAN: It must be Cyril brother…You is Cyril brother then?…is Cyril brother?…

(*Dinah looks at Jean. Pause.*) Is Cyril brother in truth…but what the arse? (*Much laughter.*)

DINAH: Listen, no offense meant to Cecil but I go tell all you something about Cyril brother. Is Cyril brother or Cecil? Is Cyril?

JEAN: Me ent know girl. Is one of them. Let me tell them. We bounce up this same Cyril.

Cyril come up by the club. We liming there a Friday night. Things was a little hard. It didn't have no ship so we wasn't down on the strip. We up the road looking to make a little change with some of the locals. And this one. He is not a regular. So we say we go hit on he. He new and looking easy to pick. He look like he have money because most of them boys round here so cheap. So I went up to him and…

DINAH (*To the audience member dubbed Cecil.*): Business today? Let we go upstairs, nuh.

JEAN (*To another audience member.*): You see how good she doing it?

DINAH: Come. (*To the rest of the audience.*) Hello, he playing shy tonight.

JEAN: You see, you see?

DINAH (*To Jean.*): You trying to set me up or what? You do it. You do it.

JEAN (*To an audience member.*): Sweetness.

DINAH: You know you could do it well.

JEAN: Sweetness, you looking for some action or what? You looking reeeaal good.

DINAH: You see, she know she thing. She know she onions.

JEAN: We ent even going upstairs. You could come by me and sleep. Not so?

DINAH: She brave. She inviting man home to spend the night with she and she have man home waiting on she, you know.

JEAN: Anyway, he went home by me.

DINAH: Don't trust him. Ask him where he was on Saturday night exactly quarter to eleven in the P.M. …..

JEAN: He spend the whole night…

DINAH: By she…

JEAN: You hear what I telling you…?

DINAH: By she…

JEAN: He went round the world and come back again.

DINAH: Eh, heh?

JEAN: He give me a blank focking cheque.

DINAH: A blank cheque, oh shit. Let we beat his arse. And Jean, you self too, ah tell you only take Yankee dollar. Ah shame for you.

JEAN: You have to live. But that was because I did done pick his pocket. (*She demonstrates how she did it.*) While he was snoring dead to this side of the world. He tell me I coulda put in on the cheque any amount I want.

DINAH: Yeah? So how much…?

JEAN: Fifty…

DINAH: Dollars…

JEAN: Thousand!

DINAH: Oh God, Jean, you does always overdo. Is greedy you greedy so…?

JEAN: But it had a catch to it. The bitch.

DINAH: You is an arse or what? It must have a catch.

JEAN: The focking account had no money in it and them half white girls in the bank watching me a kinda way…

DINAH: So you see, Mrs. Cecil, the kind of confusion your husband putting whores in town in.

JEAN: Ah want my money! (*She sings.*) You see Miss Mary. One pound.

Big and hairy.
One pound.

You see she mother.
One pound.

You see she father.
One pound…of flesh. (*They are both very drunk by this time.*)

DINAH (*Sings.*): Brown skin gyal, stay home and mind baby…

JEAN: Dinah, shut up…

DINAH (*Continues to sing and gets the audience involved. They sing a verse or two with her*): Brown skin gyal, stay home and mind baby…

JEAN: Dinah, ah warning you. Dinah!

DINAH: What Leroy father name again? The Yankee. What you use to call him? Jack on top the box.

JEAN: Jack…

DINAH (*Mocking Jean.*): Jack… (*Pause.*)
(*She sings plaintively, slowly, as if it is an old Negro Spiritual.*)

Brown skin gyal, stay home and mind baby.
Brown skin gyal, stay home and mind baby.
Ah going away in a sailing boat
And if I don't come back,
Stay home and mind baby. (*Repeat.*)

While singing this song, as the lights go to a delicate pink, Dinah dresses Jean as a pink Baby Doll masquerade character and takes her into her arms as if she was a little baby. She rocks her in her arms. During this transaction Dinah moves as if in a slow ritual.

JEAN: Mammy? Where daddy is? Who is daddy?

DINAH: Child, daddy in America. Your daddy is a big man in the Navy.

JEAN: When daddy coming to see us, mammy?

DINAH: He going to send for us soon. Any day now, he will send for us.

(*She sings another verse of 'Brown Skin Gyal'.*) And if I don't come back, throw away the damn baby. (*Silence.*) Leroy, today I have to carry you by some people who…

JEAN: What people, mammy?

DINAH: Some nice people, people who will take care…

JEAN: (*She hugs Dinah tightly.*)

Mammy, mammy. No mammy, no! (*She starts to cry and breaks from Dinah, becomes adult and walks downstage.*) Why you tell Leroy all that?

DINAH: But you must tell the child what happening. You can't just lie about the Yankee and fool up the child all the time. It was your child.

JEAN: Dinah, I couldn't mind no child that time. You know that.

DINAH: Leroy was still your responsibility. Not the responsibility of the Yankee man.

Regardless to what, not the responsibility of the Yankee.

(*Jean sobs.*) (*Dinah takes Jean in her arms.*) Come child, come.

JEAN (*Through her tears, she screams.*): Daddy! Daddy! Daddy! (*She gets louder and louder. Dinah tries to hold her and then lets her fall to the ground.*)

Dinah exits.

FADE

THE HOSPITAL

Jean rips off the headdress that was part of the Baby Doll outfit Dinah put on her earlier. She sits and wraps a piece of cloth around her left arm. Jean is in a solitary pool of light. Dinah enters, approaching her.

DINAH (*Rubbing Jean's head.*): Jean, you could have avoided this, you know.

JEAN: What is that? My life…?

DINAH: Jean, I understand, I understand (*attempting to calm her.*) You remember the very first time you reach by the club on Prince Street?

JEAN: You see me, I don't want to talk…

DINAH: Watch me. Hush, listen to me…If, as I did tell you to go home, you did go home, today you wouldn't be in this position.

JEAN: I is a big woman. I know when to go home and when not to go home. I don't want to talk about it.

DINAH: I want to talk about it, right?

JEAN: Just leave me alone. (*Pause.*)

DINAH: Jean, you, you… you don't know… All of us in the life together.

JEAN: Don't play no mother for me. I ain't looking for none. I too big for that.

DINAH: You don't have to … Try and be constructive with yourself, nah man.

JEAN: My whole life people beating up on me. Beating me up. If is not some woman, is some man or somebody who want something from me.

DINAH: I ever beat you?

JEAN: I could take care of myself.

DINAH: Look at me Jean, watch me. Watch me!

JEAN: What happen? What happen?

DINAH: Why you so? Eh? Everybody in the hospital watching. What is it Jean? Is me.

JEAN: Enough people say they care. Enough. And what?

DINAH: When you get chop on the street there, and you start bawling for your life, anybody come, eh?

JEAN: Who appoint you Queen? I don't want to hear…

DINAH: Who you run to? Who? (*Pause.*) If it wasn't for me, you would dead. Is me. Is me!

JEAN: Better you did leave me to dead.

DINAH: What?

JEAN: Because I can't work again. I can't work again. (*Pause.*) I use to be a pretty, gorgeous woman in the town, beautiful, sexy woman, eh. Now look at me. (*Pause.*) Disfigured.

DINAH: You does pray?

JEAN (*Dry smile.*): That gone out, girl. For people like me and you. You ent know that? God gone out. (*Pause.*)

DINAH: You know you could make a change with that… hand, you know.

JEAN: I not talking about that. When I call nobody don't hear. No god, no nothing.

DINAH: Watch me, watch me, Jean.

JEAN: What? Why?

DINAH: Watch me. When you come out of this place you going live with me. I don't want to see you back on the road. It ent have nothing on the road girl, I know. Nothing for nobody. Nobody.

JEAN: And who go mind me? You could mind me how I accustom living? You could mind me? You know I like pretty things and expensive clothes.

DINAH: Jean…

JEAN: Nobody never mind me yet. Not even a man. All of them promise but none of them ever mind me. You can't mind me.

DINAH: So you going back out on the road? Who want you with your hand… so?

JEAN: What wrong with my hand? You see anything wrong with my hand? Somebody tell you something the matter with my hand? Cheups! (*Pause.*)

DINAH (*She reaches out to touch Jean's hand, wanting to help.*): Look at your state.

JEAN: What you touch that for? You put something there to touch? What the fock you touch that for?

DINAH: Jean, shut up. Shut your blasted mouth.

JEAN: What you touch it for?

DINAH: What you going to do? What you going to do? You will beat me?

JEAN: Leave it alone. Just leave it alone. (*Pause.*)

DINAH: Look, you is a whore. Everybody know that. The man come to you. He offering money. What is the big thing? Go with the man. That is your work out there.

JEAN: I might be a whore…

DINAH: Listen to me, you just listen to me. Hush… If what you accustom doing is taking man, then take your man. What you making style for? You feel you will get Yankee man all the days of your life. You think they will always be around to let go money in Trinidad?

JEAN: You suppose to be my friend. Now, you hear what I have to say. You feel because I is a whore, I must go with any and everybody. That little pissin' tail man who want to pay me a little $2.00 and a little $3.00. I don't go with them kind of man. That little half a man from behind the bridge. He can't give me stick. Cave man come to town. I don't want to see he. And every time he see me, he only ridiculing me, that now the Yankees gone I have to take what I get. That good for Dorothy so. Not me. You mad or what? You crazy? For what? Eh? For what? I is Jean you know. Oh, ho. (*Pause.*) I will do for his black arse.

DINAH: What you will do? What you will do?

JEAN: My spiritual mother coming here and we going and organise something. When we done with he, he will want to know if corbeaux piss on him. Bird brain, like he. He will find out.

DINAH: Jean, I didn't come here to argue.

JEAN: Cheups! What you come for?

DINAH: You so ungrateful…

JEAN: All right, all right. Next time I get cut, leave me, let me dead. Just leave me.

DINAH: Sh! Look how everybody watching you, sssh!!

JEAN: Leave me, let me dead.

DINAH: No! I wouldn't leave you for you to dead. Not a arse of that. Ah know that is what you want. But you damn lie, you hear me. You lie! (*Pause.*) I love you like my own daughter, like my own flesh and blood. Yuh understand? And if as I did tell you, you did go home the first day I set eyes on you, this would never happen. Is a kind of love that come out for you, girl. A young bit of a girl that come inside the club. A next young girl on the road! I watch at you, Jean. And I say, 'Girl, what you doing here? Go home!' And the only thing you didn't tell me was to kiss my black arse… eh? (*Pause.*)

JEAN: So, you wasn't taking man too?

DINAH: How long you know me in the club? Eh? I is a dancer.

JEAN: Cheups!

DINAH: I is a waitress of trade. You does see me whoring with you and them dirty little almirantes it have around the town?

JEAN: I hear enough talk. You take enough (*Pause.*)

DINAH: Well, if I take enough then I have the authority to come here and sit down and talk to you. Because I know what it have out there (*Pause.*) I know out there.

JEAN: I have children to mind. I have to put food in mouth and clothes on back. I have children to mind.

DINAH: I didn't come here to argue. I didn't come here to fight with you, Jean. And I didn't bound to come here. (*Pause.*)

JEAN: You have cigarette? You bring any cigarette with you?

DINAH: Yes! (*Gives her a cigarette and lights it for her.*) How are you?

JEAN: I there. (*Pause.*) Same old Jean. Same Jean. (*Pause.*)

DINAH: When you leave here, you don't want to work in the bar? Serving drinks. Eh? If it is survival you looking for…

JEAN: Cheups!!

DINAH: Listen to me. Just listen. If it is survival you looking for out here, you don't want to just work in the bar, serving drinks? I running that bar. Popo know what happening with you. He wouldn't mind. (*Jean starts to cough.*) Cough it out, come on, cough it out. Give me the cigarette.

JEAN (*Takes it back.*): My damn cigarette. (*Pause.*)

DINAH: Answer me. (*Pause.*) Eh?

JEAN: I look like any waitress to you?

DINAH: I know you don't look like a focking waitress. But… they out for you. Jean.

Jean come and work by me. Jean, just serve drinks alone. That is all. (*Pause.*)

JEAN: You see, for me, it is always about money. I never had money yet in my life… in my life. No waitress work can't pay me. It will always be about money for me.

DINAH: How waitress work can't pay? I don't understand…

JEAN: Can't pay me. Can't live…

DINAH: You can't live off of being a waitress?

JEAN: No, can't live, can't mind. Money is the only way out. You hear me? Since I small so. We never had nothing. They always want money. Looking for money. Looking for money. For books. For school, clothes…

DINAH: Jean, Jean, I living off that work, Jean. And I mining the children with that…

JEAN: Well, that is you. Where I come from you can't mind nobody with that money and expect to live.

DINAH: So you settle. You going back out on the road?

JEAN: That is where the money is… where the money is… I will always have a price. (*Pause.*)

DINAH: You think you still have a price? (*Pause.*) Jean?

JEAN: Still have a price.

DINAH: Watch yourself good. You think you have a price? (*Pause.*) Well, what cost of a price?

JEAN: Dinah…

DINAH: Jean. I want you to stand up…

JEAN: Listen to me, Dinah. You could be a waiter, that is your business. The road I walk had nothing. It didn't have no money, no food. I didn't have no mother. It didn't have no father. All I ever wanted in my life was money and that is the only way I know how to do it. And that is how I going down. You hear me? So for me is plenty money and waitress work don't do that. You hear? It just don't do it.

(*Dinah exits.*)

FADE

BABY DOLL (The Pink Side)

Jean slowly puts on her pink Baby Doll headgear very slowly and painstakingly. She turns to the audience and takes up her shoebox. She moves in to the audience and uncovers the shoebox. She rests the cover down and takes the broken, wooden dolly out of the box. This scene is done as if an audience has gathered on the pavement to hear her.

JEAN: You know this child? This child is six months old. You never pass to see the child.

Since it born, you never bring nothing for the child. He? Wait, that is your wife? Madam, this is your husband? Well this child belong to you too, you know. This is your husband's child. Yes, your husband Mr. X from Bayshore. This child resemble you, you know. Look at the eye, nose, look at the lip. But, why you wouldn't support the child? You know what I going through to mind this child? You breed me and you leave me. The child is yours, paternity test or no paternity test. Ah don't want to hear.

He find he self in my yard, night after night. Now, tell me? What Mercedes doing in my yard? Eh?

I is a woman like my sleep. I clean out people house in the day and wash their clothes. When night come, I may go by the club a little but after that I home. Mr. Benz find he self outside my window. Mr. Cecil Brown Skin Blank Cheque Esquire climb up my board house to find his ecstasy. He come by me quick, quick, quick and gone.

He ent know how child stand up, how child navel string drop. Ent know nothing, nothing at all. But you don't know who I is? Look at me well, look at me. Well, I descend from the seed of Petite Belle Lily and Alice Sugar The Former. I trod the centuries from Na Na Yah come down. I is woman. Watch form. Ebony. From that one seed, I stand up. I grow to these proportions.

I see, it is this same boy who break in your house and tie up you and your wife and your little daughter and hold gun to your mouth, between your teeth. He is your son. But you don't know him. Because you never take care of him. You never come to see him. Now he grow like a man, he doesn't listen to me. So is jail and courthouse for him. Listen, he will terrorise you till you own up. He ent fraid the hangman cemetery, he is my son. He ent need no human right. You hang him now you need human rights. He is my son, he is your son, and you will have more and more sons to hang, necks to pop. You ask me? Mark what I tell you. Watch me good!! Watch me good!! Madam talk to him and if he know what good for him he will get to know his children, support the children.

I come now, you watching me simple, simple just so. I could turn you round you know. I could put your foot before, behind, you know. I could take away what God give you, you know. And even what he didn't give you. So hear me! Hear me! Listen to me well! Listen to my prophecy! It will come to pass. I is Jean. "Jean In Town" and if "Jean In Town" say so, is so! And if you don't want to heed I will go down deep in the bowels of hell and throw some devil shit on you. So watch it! Watch it!

(*Jean exits.*)

DANSE MACABRE (Black Baby Doll)

Enter Dinah.

Dinah is dressed in black robes reminiscent of the Midnight Robber masquerade. She has been in the underworld. She carries a coffin, the size of a shoebox in her hand. Inside the shoebox is a skeleton. This scene is done to the same pavement audience. She blows her whistle.

DINAH: Stop! Drop your keys and bow your knees and call me the Princess of the Dead. I is a woman who deliver my own self out of my mother womb. And I come down Blap! Just so. I get up and slap my own bottom and I gone. I fight man with stick, gun, bomb, hatchet, even saw. Any kinda weapon that good for war. My battle scars does heal before I get them. Young fella, you ent make me out. You ent make me out, you know. I will torment you and destroy you boy, yeah! With wine. (*She gyrates her waistline.*) Watch me good! Watch me good! Bacchanal!!!

Look! On my way down, I Ruby Rab had a confrontation with Lucy, the great Luciphobia. Flag woman at the gate. And when Lucy see me, Ruby Rab, Dinah the Dancer in a past life, the Grand Jamette, she say, "pass". She didn't want nothing to do with me. That was Lucifix! Lucifer wife. Yes! I pass Gan Gan Sarah. When she see me so she fly out she grave. First time in years. She free a lot of people if you don't know. She and Matron from Tobago, by the Silk Cotton Tree. She and Soucouyant Jane. That bloodsucker. All of them so bow to me, since I up there and that is why they send me on this mission. That if any of all you feel all you bad and could face the Grand Jamette, Princess of the Dead, all you could come now. Right now before me. Step right up! Step right up! I am the mother of the warrior musician, the Pan Man and I prepared for war, the Pan Man prepared for war, I prepare him for war. My son. Before I depart the world you have to pay up. You have to pay up! You got to pay up!!

You see me, I fight stickman from the free port to this port of Spain and then down to the main and I still fighting. Across the borders of Uropa and Merica my dragon straddle- dance the water, the agony, all the pain, and the brain drain. I never fraid any kinda stick yet. No bois could deceive these eyes. No bois could dislocate these sockets because is a long line of us you know. From Bodecia who come back now as Bodi in San Fernando.

Bodecia is a woman who tear plenty man arse loose. She never fraid Hannibal, nor the grave. Then it had my god daughter, gas station Jean. She did travel miles to stamp out corruption. All you wreak havoc with she. All you send she mad. She tell me the story up there. But she have a plan for all you, boy! I sorry for all you when that woman come back on this highway. In fact I think she here already. All who feel they is Silver Fox and could do what they want, better watch their arse. Listen to your music box. You better listen to your chutney box. You better listen, good. Who'll see, will see!! Because I is Ruby Rab, Princess of the Dead, music maker of Pan and the Pan Man and if you don't want to feel the full wrath of my tongue you better pay up! You got to pay up! Because I will embarrass from cock to cockatoo. I will peel your balls like is fig self. Yeah! I will peel your balls like a gizzard here tonight if you feel is joke we joking. Watch me good! Watch me good! Look upon me, man. Know me better!!

(*Dinah exits.*)

STEELBAND CLASH (A Pas de Deux of the Street)

Jean and Dinah are on different streets and cannot see each other. They encounter each other only at the time of the steelband clash.

JEAN (*With a San Juan All Stars flag in hand.*): Where Dinah? Look All Stars waiting for me by the Croiseé. I going. she go find me. I gone. (*She moves from stage left to right.*)

DINAH (*She appears on the other end of the stage, stage left, with a Desperadoes flag in hand.*): Well, you see your girl, swansdown coming down the side. Medal on my chest. Fancy Sailor hat on my head.

JEAN: Ramon waiting for me. I have to find he today, today in the band. Ah looking pretty?

(*Music. They both dance the Flag Woman dance.*)

DINAH: The band beating sweet. We leave on time in the yard. We leave on the hill and we coming down Piccadilly Street at about quarter to one in the afternoon.

JEAN: Coming down the road I see Jocelyn with Janet and her gang by the corner in some sailor suit. They ent even put anything new on it. They looking bad. But I looking good. My suit up to date. When Dinah see me so, she go bawl!

DINAH: Wait! (*Music stops.*) Something missing. Where Jean? She say she was going to be with us this year. She must be late.

JEAN: All you where banjo? This band can't move? Where the rhythm man? What, nobody ready? They ent even have no coffee to drink, no nothing. I need a mirror to see my costume, to fix my costume. Ramon! Come on, let us go. This is the uniform? Ramon? I thought all you say all you had uniform. We arrange this white jersey with this black pants. Eh? Nobody wearing it. This band. Oh God! Anyhow, is only because of you I here, you know. Let we go in town. I tired wait. Let us go, nah man. I find I fretting too much, sweating up myself. Where the mirror? Now is Ramon, the band, the uniform and it have man with no stick come to beat pan. Man who ent pay no dues. They know they suppose to pay me their dues. Look, all you, this band must leave San Juan for town now. Is Port of Spain! (*Music. She does a Flag*

Woman dance.) Where Dinah? Ramon, you see Dinah? Once we hit Henry Street we go meet she. You can't miss she on Charlotte Street.

DINAH: Stop! Wait! All you wait! (*Music stops.*) Hold some strain, we waiting for Jean. She suppose to come with us. To meet anywhere around here. Give me some rum there. Oh God! Yes! Good! Where you get this? Country thing? Babash, eh? (*She screws up her face.*) Good! That nice… Where this woman is? You know, when I ready to move I don't want nobody to keep me back. Where the arse is Jean? Where she is? I don't trust her, you know. Wait a minute, I ent see Ramon last night. Listen to me, fellas, my blood hot and that sun coming up, so let us move. "Iron Man"! (*Music.*) We moving. All right nuh. "Talkative", we moving. "Ocean", "Five Rivers", "Neighbour"? I go see you later, down in town, all right. (*She moves her flag and dances a vigorous Flag Woman dance, for a while.) (Pause.*) Let we take a rest here. Good. Jean go meet us here, outside home headquarters.

(*To audience.*) This music sweet, too sweet. (*Pause.*) Something must be wrong (*Pause*). So we moving. Up Henry. Across Oxford and we hitting Charlotte. (*Music gets louder, more vigorous flag dancing.*) Aye! Come, you making out that band coming down the road. That ent San Jaun All Stars? Is San Juan? Well, well, what they doing on this side? They brave. What the arse they doing on this route?

JEAN: Rhythm man! Banjo! Aye! You falling back. Keep the pace, nah man.

(*Music increases in tempo.*) Look, but that is Piggy. Oh God! Is Desperadoes? Why we band beating so slow? (*Music, more tempo.*) Look Dinah, out front. Ramon! Look! This…

DINAH: Listen, you know he? That is not a San Juan man? Aye, what you doing here?

Get to fock out this band… (*More dancing.*) Get to fock out! Out, I say! (*More dancing.*) Aye! Get to …Fight! Fight! Throw cutlash, fight! Throw cut arse… (*Pace of music increases.*)

JEAN: All you, look out! Aye! Watch the ark. Ramon, Noah's Ark full up with ammunition… Oh (*Jean throws a bottle.*) Mother arse…

DINAH (*Holds her eye.*)

BLACK OUT

DINAH: Is Jean? Oh Shit! Jean, Jean, you traitor!!!

(*Jean tries to run and hide when she sees Dinah holding her eye and doubling up on the ground.*)

(They Exit.)

EPILOGUE

"It is an indication, the Carnival is over."
- Lord Kitchener

In the blackout, Dinah, dressed in her SailorSuit, moves back to the bed in her apartment. In this scene Jean and Dinah both appear in the apartment as though they have been there all along.

DINAH: Oh God! Is you Jean. Is you.

JEAN: Is time to go, Dinah. Now is not the time to… Oh shit man… Dinah, we still have time to play. Let's go. Let us go now! What is that? You forget me?

DINAH: You pelt that bottle, Jean, (*She is losing strength*) you, you…
(*Jean hurries over*).

JEAN: Dinah, you take your pills? (*Jean is confused.*) I going and get help. Where everybody? (*She runs back into the road.*)

DINAH: Jean, Jean!! It over, it will take too long. They can't hear you. They are somewhere else, girl. In another place. They won't hear you. (*Jean hurries back to Di*nah.)

I lie down in that hospital, weeks on end and Jean you never come and see me. (*She weeps.*) Jean, weeks, Jean…

JEAN: I was coming… but… work… and them children.

DINAH: It was more than seven weeks. Oh God, Jean, seven weeks. The pain…

JEAN: Dinah, you vex with me for that?

DINAH: I vex with you since then. Since then, Jean. Jean, why you don't come out and say it, eh? The bottle that pelt… the fight… Jean, you was even looking for somewhere to hide. I see you with my one eye trying to hide from me. So you ent come to see me in the hospital because you can't face the fact that you burst my eye. Not dropsy Clementina or one of them so, you know. But is my eye you burst. Eh? (*Pause*.)

JEAN: Cyphus was the one who…

DINAH: Look, Jean! Hush!! And what is this every year coming by me? Your conscience bothering you or what?

JEAN: I could watch you. I could face you in your eye and tell you that I, Jean, didn't pelt no focking bottle. And that is that. And what is all this? Is only one eye you lose.

DINAH: I can't play no mas, child. I can't play no mas. I will be no part of your conscience, you hear me.

JEAN: Come, Dinah, let us go. We can talk all this tomorrow.

DINAH: Tomorrow and tomorrow and tomorrow. Your conscience creeping up on you or what? Petty Jamette! (*Pause.*) Now, let me sleep. I tired…

JEAN: What? Come on…

DINAH: Them days done…

JEAN: What you saying? The day still here… This is Carnival Tuesday. Let us go…

DINAH: This is Tuesday?

JEAN: Yeah…

DINAH: This day don't exist for me, Jean. It done, long time. Is midnight mass. I want to lie down. Let me lie down, nah.

JEAN: You can't lie down. We going up the road, up the road. (*She tries to pick up Dinah. She gets her to stand.*) We going up the road and we will dance. (*She tries to make her dance, she tries to dance with her.*) We must dance Dinah. (*They fall down on the floor. Jean is on top of Dinah. She tries to sit up and put Dinah's head on her lap.*) Dinah? Dinah?

DINAH: Oh God! Jean, bring one of them tablets and some water. (*Jean hurries out and rummages around for the tablets.*) I want to sleep. I have to take a rest… The pain, the pain… Look at us, eh? Like two old whore in one of them fellas calypso. Oh! Oh! (*Pause. Silence.*)

JEAN: Dinah, Dinah, Dinah!!! Oh shit! (*Shouts. She is agitated, scared.*) Neighbour, neighbour, neighbour! Dinah, Dinah? Get up! Neighbour! Neighbour! Everybody gone… (Pause.) After Ramon leave and I lose my house, you is the only one who use to take care of me, Dinah. That is why I use to come. That is why… (*She weeps with Dinah in her lap.*) Dinah, you can't dead. You know that, you can't dead. (*Pause.*) I go bury you, right? What dress you want? You ent even tell me what dress you want. We will buy a new dress. I will bury you, right? I go bear you. Me and Cyril go bury you. Right next to James. And Stallion and Marabunta and all of us will be there. And we go dance and wave flag, yes. (*She sobs uncontrollably.*) (*Pause.*) You know, Dinah, is I who burst your eye. Dinah, oh God man, get up nah man. Get up! Is I … (*Pause.*) … I who… Dinah… (*Pause.*) Oh God, Dinah, what I go do? Who I go play mas with? Who will go with me to buy cloth? When I have no food, no money, who I going by? Eh? You gone and dead. (*Music.*) You sure you don't want to get up? Look Renegades steelband passing. You don't want to go and hear them beat? (*Pause.*) You… you don't want to… dance?

FADE

THE END

Sunshine Suite
Tobago
May - October 1994

GLOSSARY

ALMIRANTES: a young prostitute whose fare is cheap.

BACCHANAL: a good time, confusion

BACRA-JOHNNY: a local white person of low economic status.

BAJAN: another name for a person who comes from Barbados.

BATONIER: stickfighter.

BODI: a long string bean.

BOIS: the stick used in the calinda or stickfight

BUBALUPS: MAYFIELD, STALLION, MARABUNTA: famous flag women

CALINDA: another word for a stickfight or stickplay.

CHANTUELLE: lead singer in the calinda band.

COMMESS: confusion (commessive the adjective) one who likes confusion.

CROISIE (QUASAY): a famous junction leading to the town of San Juan

DESPERADOES: he famous steel orchestra which started as the street gang "Dead End Kids".

FRENCH CREOLE: a member of the French Caribbean planter and land owning class who came to Trinidad from Haiti, St Lucia and Martinique in the 18th century under a Spanish administration.

GAN GAN SARAH: African slave who tried to fly back to Africa from Tobago but was unable to do so because she ate salt.

GAS STATION JEAN: Jean Miles, a famous Trinidadian public servant who tried to fight government corruption in a gas station scandal. She died in the struggle.

GLAMOURS BOYS: a street gang

HANNABAL: a famous calpysonian and stickfighter.

I IS A WHORE TOO, BIG SIX: names of famous prostitutes.

JAGABAT: low class prostitute.

JAMETTE: the Trinidad patois for the French diametre. This is the diametre or line below which most of post-emancipation Trinidad lived. Jamette became the word to describe the ordinary people of the street, the carnival reveler, the members of the calinda and stickfight bands, etc. Later, the word was used to mean prostitute, or bad woman.

MACOME MAN: homosexual

MAMAGUY: to trick or fool.

MARABUNTAS: another street gang which later became Tokyo Steel Band

MAS: masquerade.

MASTIFE: a famous badjohn who it is reported was heavily endowed.

MATRON: high priestess of traditional African religion in Tobago. She is also a traditional midwife. In 1994, she was 94 years old.

NA NA YAH: female African slave liberator.

PAN: the main instrument of the steelband (pannist - one who plays the pan).

PETIT BELLE LILY, ALICE SUGAR, RUBY RAB, BOADICEA: famous jamettes.

POOWATEE: insignificant

RENEGADES: a famous steel band or steel orchestra

ROSITA and CLEMENTINA: street women, prostitutes, made famous by Sparrow's calypso.

SAN JUAN ALL STARS: a famous steel band or steel orchestra.

.SEMP: a small yellow bird, which lives on bananas.

SOUCOUYANT: a female folk character who gets out of her skin and flies around at night in the form of a ball of fire. A bloodsucker.

SOUCOUYANT JANE: a famous soucouyant.

CARNIVAL TRADITIONS

BABY DOLL: The stickplay of the calinda or stickfight define a concept of warriorhood.

This is a warriorhood which, in the history of Trinidad Carnival, is not restricted to the male. This attitude can be traced to women of the post-emancipation Jamette Carnival and to the Baby Doll character of the Traditional masquerade in particular. The Baby Doll, a character that was popular in the thirties and forties, was a woman masquerader usually decked in a frilly dress carrying a large doll (sometimes in a box). Her action included stopping, on Carnival day, any respectably dressed gentleman and by the way of a long speech about renegade fathers she insisted that he help her mind the child, represented by the doll. It is implied in this drama of instant theatre that the gentleman, who may be on the street with his family, is the father of the child. Some researchers say that there were times when men played Baby Doll as well.

MIDNIGHT ROBBER: The Midnight Robber is one of the most beloved characters of the traditional masquerade in the Trinidad Carnival. It is believed that this character appeared sometime around the 1920's. It was usually played by men in a fancy costume which comprised a kind of cowboy trousers with breeches enhanced with beads, braid and other adornments. On his head, he carried a huge exaggerated hat (sometimes in the form of a tombstone) with fringe around the brim, making the hat crown-like. His shoes were a wire structure of some animal, which moved as he walked with his characteristic long steps. This rather intriguing costume was completed with a long flowing cape on which were painted or embroidered skulls and cross bones and other signs of death and destruction. In his hands, he carried a gun and a wooden cash box. Around his waist he stuck more guns in a cartridge belt and he blew an ever-present whistle which hung from around his neck. On Carnival days, when he accosted bystanders on the street, the speech that emanated from his mouth like shots from an automatic pistol was no less extravagant than his costume and rhythmic dance movements. You had to give him a few coins to get this fearsome character to move on down the street. For he is the ultimate bad man, full of empty threats and the wildest implausible boasting possible. There is nothing he has not done. He is the one who "at the age of two, drowned my grandmother in a spoonful of water". Over the years, this character had almost disappeared from the Carnival but within recent time he is enjoying a welcomed revival.

SAILOR/FANCY SAILOR: Just as the Baby Doll character is about keeping the truth, the Sailor/Fancy Sailor is about Yankee Imperialism. In the 1930's, steel drums were brought to the island by Americans who went there to refine oil, a natural resource found on the island. The pan, the musical instrument created from these, is the main instrument of the steel band. However, what began at this time, among the ordinary people, was a fascination with things American. By the 1940's, World War II had broken out and Trinidad became a place for American military bases. There was a Jungle Warfare School set up on the island. The locals responded to this development through the calypso and the carnival. The sailor is a mas' portrayal, popularised mainly by the steelbands. Called "bad behaviour sailors", these characters came out in their hundreds, in their simple white costumes year after year and displayed the freedom and "gay abandon" which they observed the "drunken" yankee sailors enjoyed on the streets of Port of Spain. The yankees, of course, had U.S. dollars to spend on wine, women and song. This attitude of free expression so captivated the imagination of the masqueraders that pretty soon the plain sailor suit was not enough to capture the spirit of celebration and emancipation that is the carnival. They began to decorate the basic white costume and developed many appropriate dances. So today we have the Fancy Sailor and King Sailor, which can explore Japanese, African, even environmental and other themes through designs built on to a sailor suit. The Fancy Sailor, created by the ordinary people of Trinidad and Tobago, has added a new dimension to surrealist art.

ABOUT THE AUTHOR

Tony Hall is a playwright and actor who has worked extensively in Western Canada and with the Trinidad Theatre Workshop. He has also worked with Banyan Limited in developing television for the Caribbean. In 1990, Tony and Errol Fabien launched The Lordstreet Theatre Company with the jouvay mas *A Band on Drugs.* Mr. Hall has been Visiting Artist in Residence at Trinity College, Hartford, Connecticut since 1998.

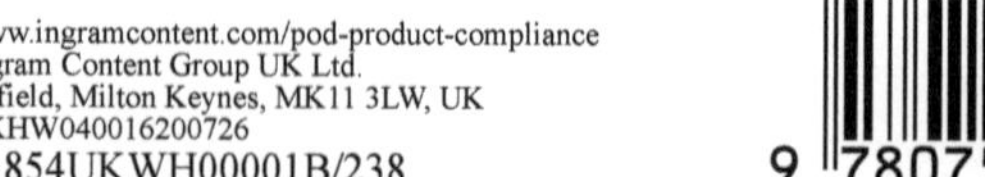

www.ingramcontent.com/pod-product-compliance
Ingram Content Group UK Ltd.
Pitfield, Milton Keynes, MK11 3LW, UK
UKHW040016200726
13854UKWH00001B/238

9 780759 687974